First
Arabic Words

Illustrated by David Melling

OXFORD
UNIVERSITY PRESS

For Bosiljka, Branko and Igor Sunajko.
D.M.

OXFORD
UNIVERSITY PRESS

Great Clarendon Street, Oxford OX2 6DP

Oxford University Press is a department of the University of Oxford.
It furthers the University's objective of excellence in research, scholarship,
and education by publishing worldwide in

Oxford New York

Auckland Cape Town Dar es Salaam Hong Kong Karachi
Kuala Lumpur Madrid Melbourne Mexico City Nairobi
New Delhi Shanghai Taipei Toronto

With offices in

Argentina Austria Brazil Chile Czech Republic France Greece
Guatemala Hungary Italy Japan Poland Portugal Singapore
South Korea Switzerland Thailand Turkey Ukraine Vietnam

Oxford is a registered trade mark of Oxford University Press
in the UK and in certain other countries

Illustrations copyright © David Melling 1999
Text copyright © Oxford University Press 1999

Database right Oxford University Press (maker)

First published as First Book of Words 1999
First published as First Arabic Words 2009

English words compiled by Neil Morris
Arabic translation by Lingo 24, Dr Basil Mustafa, Hanan Omar

British Library Cataloguing in Publication Data available

ISBN: 978-0-19-911135-0

3 5 7 9 10 8 6 4 2

Paper used in the production of this book is a natural,
recyclable product made from wood grown in sustainable forests.
The manufacturing process conforms to the environmental
regulations of the country of origin.

Printed in Singapore

The Arabic translations reflect formal usage. All efforts have been made to ensure that these translations are accurate and
appropriate. If you have any further language queries, please visit our website at www.askoxford.com.

Contents

أنت وأنا	4-5	You and Me
في المنزل	6- 7	At Home
في الطريق إلى المدرسة	8- 9	On the Way to School
فصلنا	10-11	Our Classroom
اللعب بالألوان	12-13	Fun with Colours
المهن	14-15	Professions
حدث ذات مرة	16-17	Once Upon a Time
في المتجر	18-19	At the Supermarket
فترة الغداء	20-21	Lunchtime
فترة اللعب!	22-23	Playtime!
في المزرعة	24-25	On the Farm
على الشاطئ	26-27	At the Seaside
حفلة عيد ميلاد	28-29	Birthday Party
حيوانات مسلية	30-31	Amusing Animals
في الحمام	32-33	In the Bathroom
تصبحون على خير!	34-35	Goodnight!
قاموسي المصور	36-37	My Picture Dictionary
عد معي ! ٣ ٢ ١	38-39	Count with Me! 123
الأشكال	40-41	Shapes
الأضداد	42-43	Opposites
الجو	44	Weather
الوقت	45	Time
الفهرس	46-48	Index

أنت وأنا

You and Me

صدر
chest

رجل
leg

إصبع القدم
toe

قدم
foot

مرفق
elbow

ردف
bottom

ظهر
back

إصبع اليد
finger

بطن
tummy

ركبة
knee

يد
hand

شعر
hair

ذراع
arm

أكتاف /
عواتق /
مناكب
shoulders

رأس
head

وجه
face

وجنة / خد
cheek

أذن
ear

عين
eye

فم
mouth

ذقن
chin

لسان
tongue

أسنان
teeth

أنف
nose

عنق
neck

ولد / صبي
boy

بنت / صبية
girl

في المنزل

At Home

سقف
roof

بوابة
gate

سلة المهملات
dustbin/
(US) trashcan

سلم
stairs

مدخنة
chimney

سياج
fence

مرآب
garage

نافذة / شباك
window

باب
door

6

كلب
dog

قطة
cat

أرنب
rabbit

عنكبوت
spider

قوقع
snail

رسائل /
خطابات
letters

حقيبة البريد
postbag

ورقة (نبات)
leaf

زهرة
flower

شجرة
tree

في الطريق إلى المدرسة
On the Way to School

رصيف
pavement

عمود الإنارة
lamp post

ساحة لعب /
ملعب
playground

شارع
street

معبر المشاة
zebra crossing /
(US) crosswalk

مدرسة
school

إشارات المرور
traffic lights

محل / دكان
shop

كنيسة
church

دراجة
bicycle

سيارة
car

حافلة
bus

دراجة بخارية /
دراجة نارية
motorbike

سيارة إطفاء
fire engine

شاحنة
truck

طائرة مروحية
helicopter

سيارة إسعاف
ambulance

طائرة
plane

فصلنا
Our Classroom

حقيبة مدرسية
school bag

كتاب
book

علبة الغداء
lunch box

سبورة
blackboard

طباشير
chalk

الكرة الأرضية
globe

مكتب / منضدة
desk

مغناطيس
magnet

صندوق الزبالة
bin

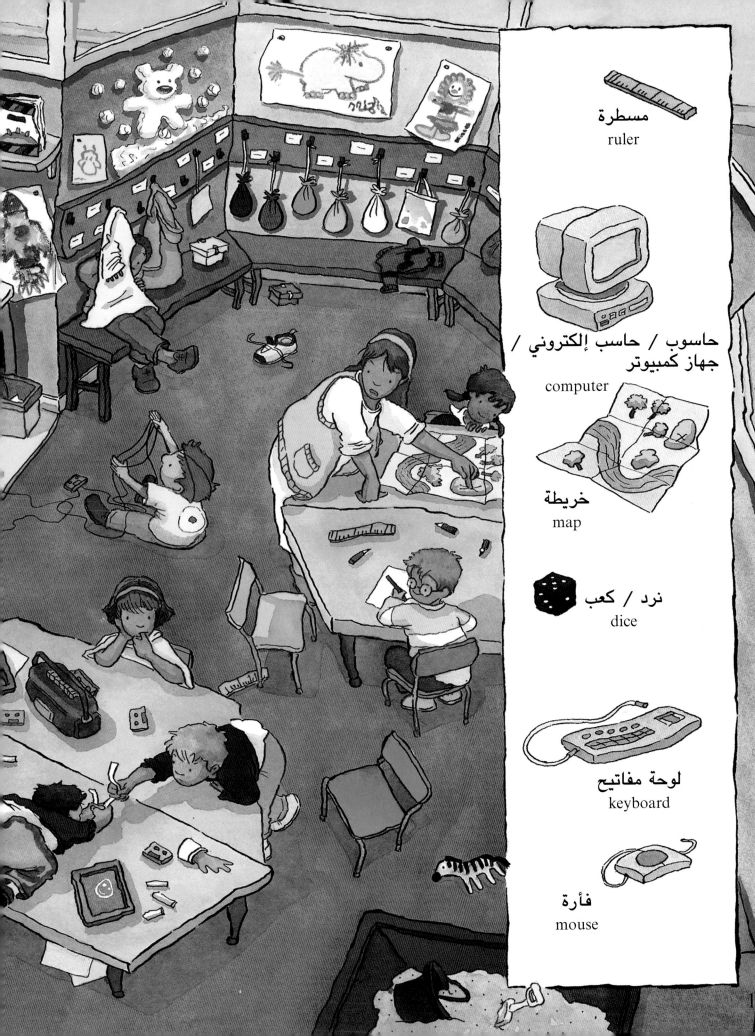

مسطرة
ruler

حاسوب / حاسب إلكتروني / جهاز كمبيوتر
computer

خريطة
map

نرد / كعب
dice

لوحة مفاتيح
keyboard

فأرة
mouse

اللعب بالألوان
Fun with Colours

أسود
black

أزرق
blue

بني
brown

أخضر
green

رمادي / رصاصي
grey

برتقالي
orange

قرنفلي / وردي / زهري
pink

أرجواني
purple

أحمر
red

أبيض
white

أصفر
yellow

12

رداء عمل /
بزة عمل /
ثوب عمل
overalls

غراء / صمغ
glue

صورة زيتية
painting

فرشاة الرسم
paintbrush

ألوان الرسم
paints

قلم رصاص
pencil

ورق / أوراق
paper

مقص
scissors

قلم لباد
felt-tip pen

حامل
easel

13

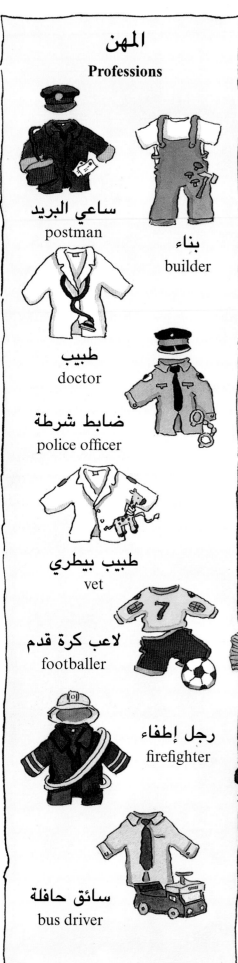

المهن
Professions

ساعي البريد
postman

بناء
builder

طبيب
doctor

ضابط شرطة
police officer

طبيب بيطري
vet

لاعب كرة قدم
footballer

رجل إطفاء
firefighter

سائق حافلة
bus driver

سائق قطار
train driver

نجم الغناء
pop star

طيار
pilot

راقص
dancer

غواص
diver

طاهي / طباخ
cook

رائد فضاء
astronaut

مسعف
lifeguard

15

حدث ذات مرة
Once Upon a Time

ديناصور
Dinosaurs

قبل ٢٠٠ مليون عام مضت
200 million years ago

تيرانوسورس ريكس
Tyrannosaurus Rex

ستيجوصور
Stegosaurus

ديبلودوكس
Diplodocus

هيكل التراسيراتوبس
Triceratops skeleton

أُحفور / حفرية
fossil

عظمة
bone

في المتجر
At the Supermarket

عربة البضائع
trolley

سـلة
basket

آلة تسجيل النقد /
الصندوق
till

خبز
bread

كعكة محلاة
bun

مربى
jam

حبّ / حبوب /
حبوب الإفطار
cereal

بطاطس
potatoes

سجق
sausages

مكرونة سباجتي
spaghetti

حليب
milk

زبادي
yoghurt

جبن
cheese

بيض
eggs

تفاح
apple

موز
banana

برتقال
orange

طماطم
tomato

جزر
carrot

خس
lettuce

19

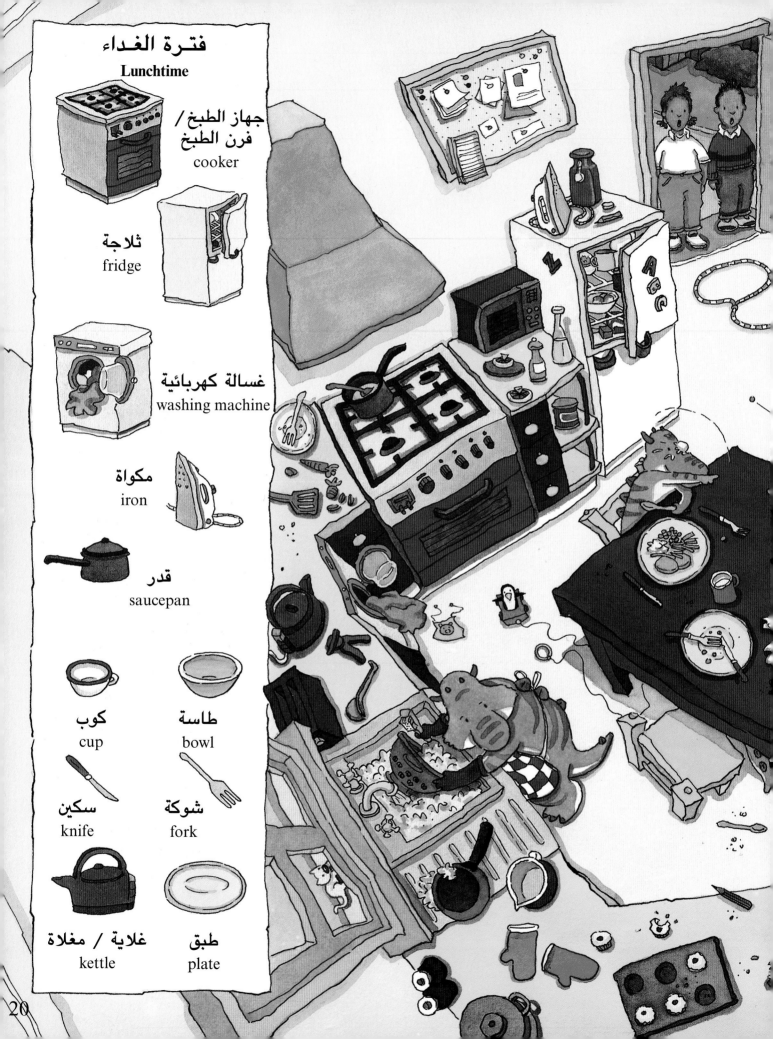

فترة الغداء
Lunchtime

جهاز الطبخ /
فرن الطبخ
cooker

ثلاجة
fridge

غسالة كهربائية
washing machine

مكواة
iron

قدر
saucepan

كوب
cup

طاسة
bowl

سكين
knife

شوكة
fork

غلاية / مغلاة
kettle

طبق
plate

طبق الفنجان
saucer

ملعقة
spoon

كرسي
chair

إبريق الشاي
teapot

مخدة /
وسادة واقية
cushion

أريكة
sofa

مجسم الصوت
stereo

مائدة /
طاولة
table

تلفاز /
جهاز التلفزيون
television

مكنسة كهربائية
vacuum cleaner

فترة اللعب !
Playtime!

بيت الدمية
doll's house

دمية
doll

لعبة
game

سيارة سباق
racing car

إنسان آلي
robot

لعبة تركيب الصور
jigsaw puzzle

دمية الدب
teddy

لعبة القطار
train set

22

طبل
drum

قيثارة
guitar

لوحة مفاتيح
keyboard

مكبر الصوت
microphone

بوق
trumpet

مزمار
recorder

صَنج
cymbals

أجراس
bells

الدف
tambourine

23

في المزرعة
On the Farm

حصان
horse

دجاجة
chicken

ديك
cockerel

بطة
duck

وزة
goose

خروف
sheep

عنزة / ماعز
goat

بقرة
cow

24

جرار زراعي
tractor

جدول مائي
stream

قنطرة / جسر
bridge

حقل
field

غابة
forest

تبن
hay

ربوة / تلّ
hill

فزاعة
scarecrow

على الشاطئ
At the Seaside

كرة
ball

دلو
bucket

مجراف
spade

كرسي قابل للطّي
deckchair

مظلة
umbrella

كريم شمس
suncream/ (US) sunscreen

منحدر
slide

نواسة / أرجوحة
see-saw

أرجوحة / مرجوحة
swing

سفينة
ship

منارة
lighthouse

قلعة رملية
sandcastle

نورس البحر
seagull

صدفة
shell

سرطان البحر
crab

أخطبوط
octopus

قنديل البحر
starfish

طحلب بحري
seaweed

حفلة عيد ميلاد
Birthday Party

بطاقة عيد ميلاد
birthday card

شمعة
candle

مُنطاد
balloon

هدية
present

راية
streamer

صافرة ورقية
party blower

قبعة حفلة
party hat

صولجان /
عصا الساحر
wand

مهرج
clown

حلوى
sweets

شطيرة
sandwich

بيتزا
pizza

آيس كريم
ice cream

شوكولاتة
chocolate

بسكوت
biscuit

ماصة
straw

مشروب
drink

كعك / كيك
cake

حيوانات مسلية
Amusing Animals

فيل
elephant

تمساح
crocodile

زرافة
giraffe

سمكة
fish

فرس النهر
hippopotamus

كنغر
kangaroo

قرد
monkey

كوال
koala

فَأر
mouse

فظ / فيل البحر
walrus

بـبغاء
parrot

بطريق
penguin

نمر
tiger

حمار وحشي
zebra

البندا
panda

وحيد القرن
rhinoceros

31

في الحمام
In the Bathroom

ثوب
dress

سترة
jacket

كنزة صوفية
jumper/
(US) sweater

سراويل قصيرة
shorts

سراويل داخلية
pants

قميص
shirt

أحذية
shoes

تنورة
skirt

جوارب
socks

سروال
trousers

تي شيرت
T-shirt

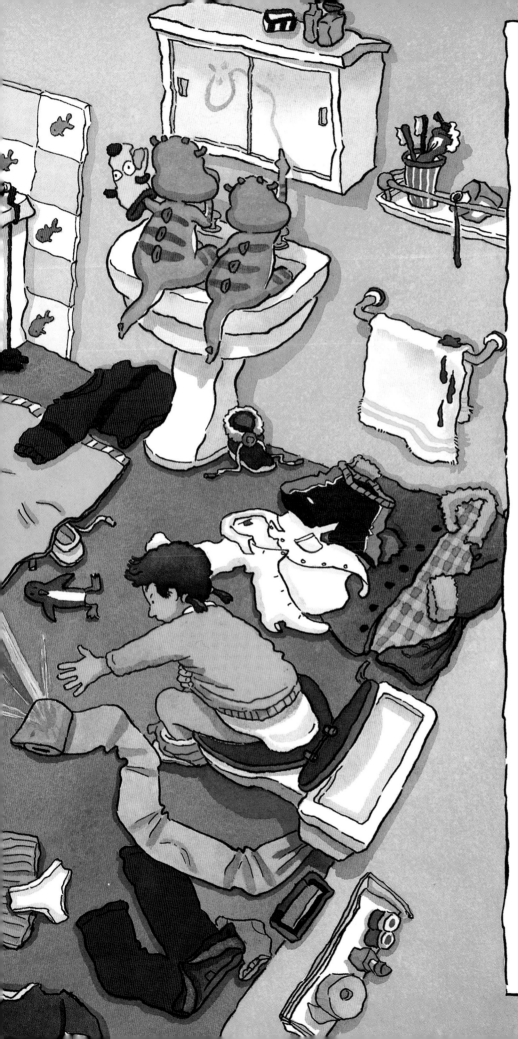

حوض
basin

مغطس
bath

فانلة
flannel

مرآة
mirror

مرشة الإغتسال
shower

صابونة / صابون
soap

إسفنجة
sponge

مرحاض
toilet

ورق المرحاض
toilet paper

فرشة أسنان
toothbrush

معجون أسنان
toothpaste

منشفة
towel

تصبحون على خير!
Goodnight!

دولاب الملابس
wardrobe

ستائر
curtains

مصباح
lamp

منضدة جانب السرير
bedside table

رداء النوم
pyjamas

ثوب النوم
nightdress

وسادة
pillow

سرير
bed

بطانية
blanket

خزانة ملابس
chest

كتاب قصص
storybook

قلعة
castle

ملك   ملكة
king   queen

جني
genie

المصباح السحري
magic lamp

تنين
dragon

مارد
giant

قاموسي المصور
My Picture Dictionary

Match the words with the pictures

نملة
ant

بيضة
egg

سمكة
fish

جرس
bell

طائرة مروحية
helicopter

كلب
dog

لاعب خفة
juggler

ملك
king

ملكة
queen

أخطبوط
octopus

عربة
van

خنفساء
ladybird

دمية
puppet

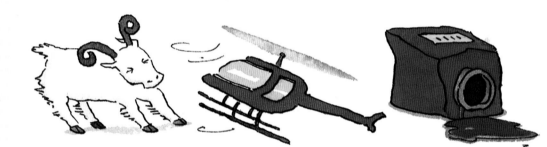

فأر
mouse

مسمار
nail

يسروع/دودة الفراشة
caterpillar

مظلة
umbrella

خاتم
ring

أشعة إكس
X-ray

يخت
yacht

جوارب
socks

نمر
tiger

حبر
ink

ساعة يد
watch

حمار وحشي
zebra

عنزة/ماعز
goat

صفر ٠
0 zero

واحد ١
1 one

إثنان ٢
2 two

ثلاثة ٣
3 three

أربعة ٤
4 four

خمسة ٥
5 five

ستة ٦
6 six

سبعة ٧
7 seven

ثمانية ٨
8 eight

تسعة ٩
9 nine

عشرة ١٠
10 ten

الأول
first

الثاني
second

الثالث
third

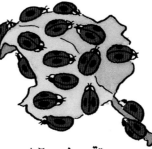

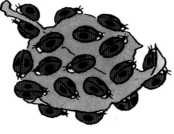

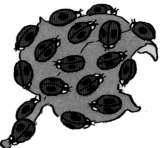

إحدى عشر ١١	إثنى عشر ١٢	ثلاثة عشر ١٣
11 eleven	12 twelve	13 thirteen

أربعة عشر ١٤	خمسة عشر ١٥	ستة عشر ١٦	سبعة عشر ١٧
14 fourteen	15 fifteen	16 sixteen	17 seventeen

ثمانية عشر ١٨	تسعة عشر ١٩	عشرون ٢٠
18 eighteen	19 nineteen	20 twenty

الرابع
fourth

الخامس
fifth

الأخير
last

الأشكال
Shapes

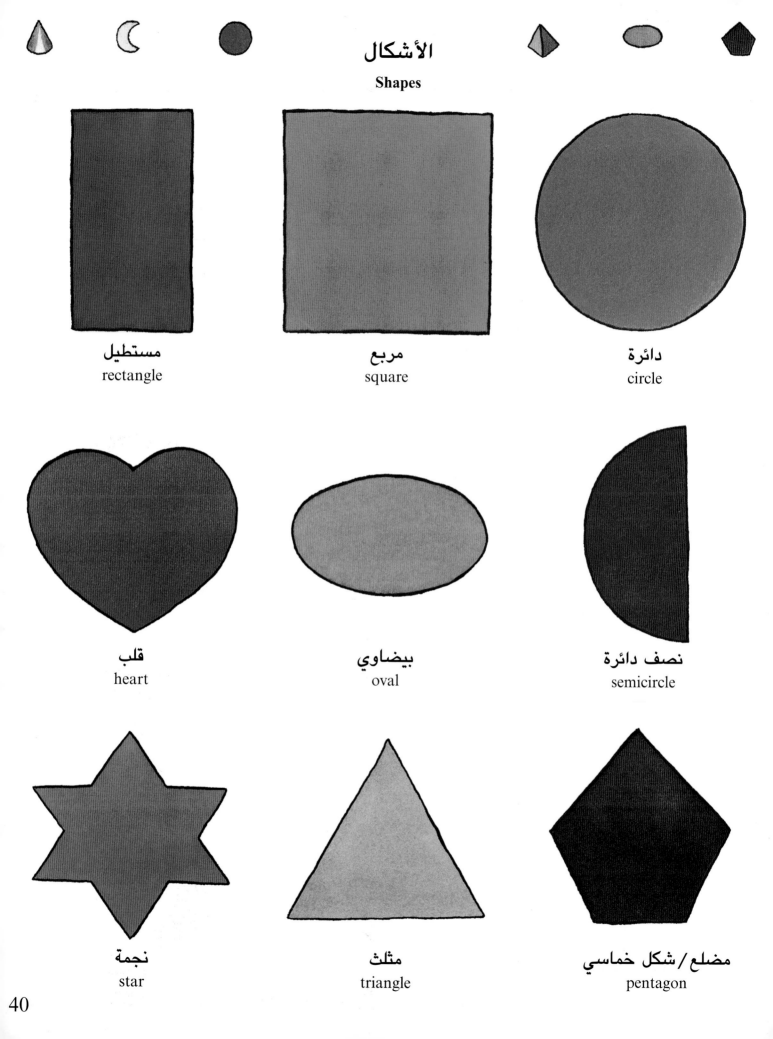

مستطيل
rectangle

مربع
square

دائرة
circle

قلب
heart

بيضاوي
oval

نصف دائرة
semicircle

نجمة
star

مثلث
triangle

مضلع/شكل خماسي
pentagon

40

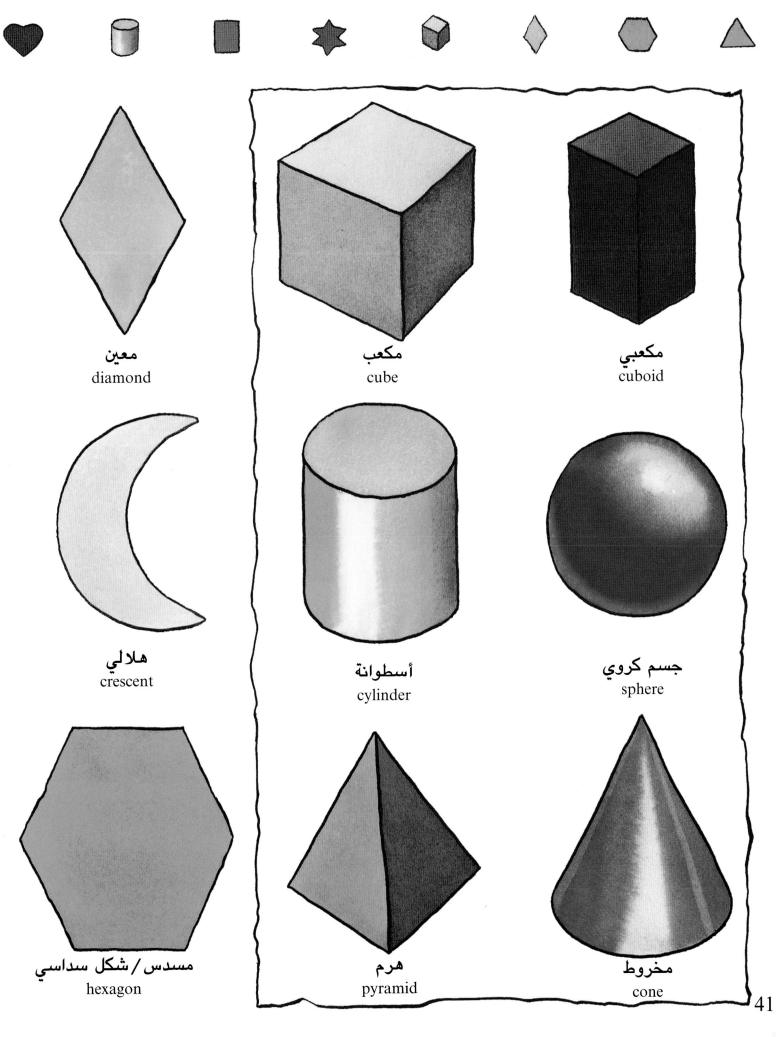

معين
diamond

مكعب
cube

مكعبي
cuboid

هلالي
crescent

أسطوانة
cylinder

جسم كروي
sphere

مسدس/شكل سداسي
hexagon

هرم
pyramid

مخروط
cone

41

كبير صغير	نظيف قذر
big small	clean dirty
بدين نحيف	ممتلئ فارغ
fat thin	full empty
مرتفع منخفض	ساخن بارد
high low	hot cold
جديد قديم	مفتوح مغلق
new old	open closed

42

مُظلِم / مُعتِم	مُضاء	سريع	بطيء
dark	light	fast	slow

سعيد	حزين	ثقيل	خفيف
happy	sad	heavy	light

طويل	قصير	أكثر	أقل
long	short	more	less

شبيه	مختلف	رطب	جاف
same	different	wet	dry

43

غائم
cloudy

مشمس
sunny

ممطر / مطير
rainy

ثلجي
snowy

عاصف
windy

ضبابي
foggy

44

الساعة الثامنة
eight o'clock

الساعة العاشرة
ten o'clock

الساعة الثانية عشر
twelve o'clock

الساعة الثانية
two o'clock

الساعة الرابعة
four o'clock

الساعة السادسة
six o'clock

45

INDEX

Note: All masculine (مذ) and feminine (م) forms are included.

ENGLISH: A B C

ambulance	9
ant	36
apple	19
arm	4
astronaut	15
back	4
ball	26
balloon	28
banana	19
basin	33
basket	18
bath	33
bed	34
bedside table	34
bell	36
bells	23
bicycle	9
big	42
bin	10
birthday card	28
biscuit	29
black	12
blackboard	10
blanket	34
blue	12
bone	16
book	10
bottom	4
bowl	20
boy	5
bread	18
bridge	25
brown	12
bucket	26
builder	14
bun	18
bus	9
bus driver	14
cake	29
candle	28
car	9
carrot	19
cash register	18
castle	35
cat	7
caterpillar	36
cave	17
cave painting	17
cereal	18
chair	21
chalk	10
cheek	5
cheese	19
chest (body)	4
chest (furniture)	34
chicken	24
chimney	6
chin	5
chocolate	29
church	8
circle	40
clean	42
closed	42
cloudy	44
cock	24
coins	17
cold	42
computer	11
cone	41
cook	15

cooker	20
cow	24
crab	27
crescent	41
crocodile	30
cube	41
cuboid	41
cup	20
curtains	34
cushion	21
cylinder	41
cymbals	23

D E F

dancer	15
dark	43
deckchair	26
desk	10
diamond	41
dice	11
different	43
dinosaurs	16
Diplodocus	16
dirty	42
diver	15
doctor	14
dog	7, 36
doll	22
doll's house	22
door	6
dragon	35
dress	32
drink	29
drum	23
dry	43
duck	24
dustbin	6
ear	5
easel	13
egg	36
eggs	19
eight	38
eighteen	39
elbow	4
elephant	30
eleven	39
empty	42
eye	5
face	5
fast	43
fat	42
felt-tip pen	13
fence	6
field	25
fifteen	39
fifth	39
finger	4
fire	17
fire engine	9
firefighter	14
first	38
fish	30, 36
five	38
flannel	33
flint	17
flower	7
foggy	44
foot	4
footballer	14
forest	25
fork	20
fossil	16

four	38
fourteen	39
fourth	39
fridge	20
full	42

G H I

game	22
garage	6
gate	6
genie	35
giant	35
giraffe	30
girl	5
globe	10
glue	13
goat	24, 36
goose	24
green	12
grey	12
guitar	23
hair	4
hand	4
happy	43
hay	25
head	4
heart	40
heavy	43
helicopter	9, 36
hexagon	41
high	42
hill	25
hippopotamus	30
horse	24
hot	42
ice cream	29
ink	36
iron	20

J K L

jacket	32
jam	18
jigsaw puzzle	22
juggler	36
jumper	32
kangaroo	30
kettle	20
keyboard (music)	23
keyboard (PC)	11
king	35, 36
knee	4
knife	20
koala	30
ladybird	36
lamp	34
lamp post	8
last	39
leaf	7
leg	4
less	43
letters	7
lettuce	19
lifeguard	15
light	43
lighthouse	27
long	43
low	42
lunch box	10

M N O

magic lamp	35
magician	28

magnet	10
map	11
microphone	23
milk	19
mirror	33
monkey	30
more	43
motorbike	9
mouse (animal)	31, 36
mouse (PC)	11
mouth	5
nail	37
neck	5
new	42
nightdress	34
nine	38
nineteen	39
nose	5
octopus	27, 37
old	42
one	38
open	42
orange (colour)	12
orange (fruit)	19
oval	40
overall	13

P Q R

paintbrush	13
painting	13
paints	13
panda	31
pants	32
paper	13
parrot	31
party blower	28
party hat	28
pavement	8
pencil	13
penguin	31
pentagon	40
Pharaoh	17
pillow	34
pilot	15
pink	12
pizza	29
plane	9
plate	20
playground	8
police officer	14
pop star	15
postbag	7
postman	14
potatoes	18
pottery	17
present	28
puppet	37
purple	12
pyjamas	34
pyramid (Egypt)	17
pyramid (shape)	41
queen	35, 37
rabbit	7
racing car	22
rainy	44
recorder	23
rectangle	40
red	12
rhinoceros	31
ring	37
robot	22
roof	6

ruler 11

S T U

sad 43
same 43
sandcastle 27
sandwich 29
saucepan 20
saucer 21
sausages 18
scarecrow 25
school 8
school bag 10
scissors 13
seagull 27
seaweed 27
second 38
see-saw 26
semi-circle 40
seven 38
seventeen 39
sheep 24
shell 27
ship 27
shirt 32
shoes 32
shop 8
short 43
shorts 32
shoulders 4
shower 33
six 38
sixteen 39
skirt 32
slide 26
slow 43
small 42
snail 7
snowy 44
soap 33
socks 32, 37
sofa 21
soldier 17
spade 26
spaghetti 18
sphere 41
sphinx 17
spider 7
sponge 33
spoon 21
square 40
stairs 6
star 40
starfish 27
Stegosaurus 16
stereo 21
storybook 35
straw 29
stream 25
streamer 28
street 8
suncream 26
sunny 44
sweets 29
swing 26
table 21
tambourine 23
teapot 21
teddy 22
teeth 5
television 21
ten 38
thin 42
third 37
thirteen 39
three 38

tiger 31, 37
time 45
toe 4
toilet 33
toilet paper 33
tomato 19
tongue 5
toothbrush 33
toothpaste 33
towel 33
tractor 25
traffic lights 8
train driver 15
train set 22
tree 7
triangle 40
Triceratops 16
Triceratops skeleton 16
trolley 18
trousers 32
truck 9
trumpet 23
T-shirt 32
tummy 4
twelve 39
twenty 39
two 38
Tyrannosaurus Rex 16
umbrella 26, 37

V W

vacuum cleaner 21
van 37
vet 14
walrus 31
wand 28
wardrobe 34
washing machine 20
watch 37
wet 43
white 12
window 6
windy 44

X Y Z

X-ray 37
yacht 37
yellow 12
yoghurt 19
zebra 31, 37
zebra crossing 8
zero 38

ARABIC:

أ
إبريق الشاي (مذ) 21
أبو الهول (مذ) 17
أبيض / بيضاء (مذ/م) 12
إثنى عشر/اثني عشر (مذ/م) 39
إثنان / إثنتان (مذ/م) 38
أجراس (م) 23
أحد عشر / إحدى عشر(مذ/م) 39
أحذية (م) 32
أحفور(مذ) 16
أحمر/ حمراء (مذ/م) 12
أخضر/ خضراء (مذ/م) 12
أخطبوط (مذ) 36, 27
الأخير/ الأخيرة (مذ/م) 39
أذن (م) 5
أربع عشر/ أربعة عشر (مذ/م) 39
أربع/ أربعة (مذ/م) 38
أرجواني/ أرجوانية (مذ/م) 12
أرجوحة (م) 26
أرنب (مذ) 7
أريكة (م) 21
أزرق/ زرقاء (مذ/م) 12

أسطوانة (م) 19
إسفنجة (م) 25
أسنان (م) 5
أسود/ سوداء (م) 12
إشارات المرور (م) 8
أشعة إكس (م) 37
إصبع القدم (مذ) 4
إصبع اليد (مذ) 4
أصفر/ صفراء (مذ/م) 12
أكتاف (م) 4
الباندا (مذ) 31
آلة تسجيل النقد (م) 18
ألوان الرسم (م) 11
إنسان آلي (مذ) 22
أنف (مذ) 5
الأشكال (م) 40
الأضداد (م) 42
الأواني الفخارية (م) 17
الأول/ الأولى (مذ/م) 38
أوراق (م) ( ) جمع=plural 13
آيس كريم (مذ) 29

ب
باب (مذ) 6
بارد/ باردة (مذ/م) 42
ببغاء (مذ) 31
بدين/ بدينة (مذ/م) 42
برتقال (الفاكهة) (مذ) 19
برتقالي/ برتقالية (اللون) (مذ/م) 12
بزة عمل (م) 13
بسكوت (مذ) 29
بطاطس (م) 18
بطاقة عيد ميلاد (م) 28
بطانية (م) 34
بطة (م) 24
بطريق (مذ) 31
بطن (مذ) 4
بطيء/ بطيئة (مذ/م) 43
بقرة (م) 24
بناء/ بناءة (مذ/م) 14
بنت (م) 5
بني/ بنية (مذ/م) 12
بوابة (م) 6
بوق (م) 23
بيت الدمية (مذ) 22
بيتزا (م) 29
بيض (مذ) 19
بيضاوي/ بيضاوية (مذ/م) 40
بيضة (م) 36

ت
تبن (مذ) 25
التراسيراتوبس (مذ) 16
تسع عشر/ تسعة عشر (مذ/م) 39
تسع/ تسعة (مذ/م) 39
تفاح (مذ) 19
تلّ (مذ) 25
تلفاز (مذ) 21
تمساح (مذ) 30
تنورة (م) 32
تنين (مذ) 37
تي شيرت (مذ) 32
تيرانوسورس ريكس (مذ) 16

ث
الثالث/ الثالثة (مذ/م) 38
الثاني/ الثانية (مذ/م) 38
ثقيل/ ثقيلة (مذ/م) 43
ثلاث عشر/ثلاثة عشر (مذ/م) 39
ثلاث / ثلاثة (مذ/م) 38
ثلاجة (م) 20
ثُلجي (مذ) 44
ثمان عشر/ ثمانية عشر (مذ/م) 39
ثمان/ ثمانية (مذ/م) 38
ثوب (مذ) 32
ثوب النوم (مذ) 34

ج
جاف/ جافة (مذ/م) 43

جبن (مذ) 19
جدول مائي (م) 25
جديد / جديدة (مذ/م) 42
جرار زراعي (مذ) 25
جرس (مذ) 8
جزر (مذ) 19
جسر (مذ) 8
جسم كروي (مذ) 41
جندي (مذ) 17
جني/ جنية (مذ/م) 35
جهاز التلفزيون (مذ) 21
جهاز الطبخ (مذ) 20
جهاز كمبيوتر (مذ) 11
جوارب (م) 32,37

ح
حاسب إلكتروني (مذ) 11
حاسوب (مذ) 11
حافلة (م) 9
حامل (مذ) 13
حبّ (مذ) 18
حبر (م) 11
حبوب (م) 18
حبوب الإفطار (م) 18
حجر (مذ) 17
حزين/ حزينة (مذ/م) 43
حصان (مذ) 24
حفرية (م) 16
حقل (مذ) 25
حقيبة البريد (م) 7
حقيبة مدرسية (م) 10
حلوى (م) 29
حليب (م) 19
حمار وحشي (مذ) 37, 31
حوض (مذ) 33

خ
خاتم (مذ) 37
الخامس/ الخامسة (مذ/م) 39
خبز (مذ) 18
خد (مذ) 5
خروف (مذ) 24
خريطة (م) 11
خس (مذ) 19
خطابات (مذ) 7
خفيف/ خفيفة (مذ/م) 43
خمس عشر/ خمسة عشر (مذ/م) 39
خمس/ خمسة (مذ/م) 38
خنفساء (م) 36

د
دائرة (م) 40
دجاجة (م) 24
دراجة (م) 9
دراجة بخارية (م) 9
دراجة نارية (م) 9
الدف (مذ) 23
دكان (مذ) 8
دلو (مذ) 26
دمية (م) 22
دمية الدب (م) 22
دودة الفراشة (م) 37
دولاب الملابس (مذ) 34
ديبلودوكس (مذ) 16

ذ
ذراع (م) 4
ذقن (مذ) 5

ر
رائد فضاء (مذ) 15
الرابع/ الرابعة (مذ/م) 38
رأس (مذ) 4
راقص/ راقصة (مذ/م) 15
راية (م) 28
ربوة (م) 25
رجل (مذ) 4
رجل إطفاء (مذ) 14
رداء النوم (مذ) 34
رداء عمل (مذ) 13

مظلة (م) 26, 37
معبر المشاة (مذ) 8
مُعتم (مذ) 43
معجون أسنان (مذ) 33
معين (مذ) 41
مغطس (مذ) 33
مغلاة (م) 20
مغلق / مغلقة (مذ/م) 42
مغناطيس (مذ) 10
مفتوح / مفتوحة (مذ/م) 42
مقص (مذ) 13
مكبر الصوت (مذ) 23
مكتب (مذ) 10
مكرونة سباجتي (م) 18
مكعب (مذ) 41
مكعبي (مذ) 41
مكنسة كهربائية (م) 21
مكواة (م) 20
ملعب (مذ) 8
ملعقة (م) 21
ملك (مذ) 35, 36
ملكة (م) 35, 37
ممتلئ / ممتلئة (مذ/م) 42
ممطر (مذ) 44
منارة (م) 27
مناكب (م) 4
منحدر (مذ) 26
منخفض / منخفضة (مذ/م) 42
منشفة (م) 33
منضدة (م) 10
مُنطاد (مذ) 28
مهرج (مذ) 28
موز (مذ) 19
ن
نار (م) 17
نافذة (م) 6
نجم / نجمة)الغناء((مذ/م) 15
نجمة (م) 40
نحيف / نحيفة (مذ/م) 42
نرد (مذ) 11
نصف دائرة (مذ) 40
ظيف / نظيفة (مذ/م) 42
نمر (مذ) 37, 31
نملة (م) 36
نواسة (م) 26
نورس البحر (مذ) 27
هـ
هدية (م) 28
هرم (الشكل) (مذ) 41
هرم (مصر) (مذ) 17
هلال (مذ) 41
هيكل عظمي (مذ) 16
و
واحد (مذ) 38
وجنة (م) 5
وجه (مذ) 5
وحيد القرن (مذ) 31
وردي (اللون) (مذ) 12
ورق (مذ) (جمع=plural) 13
ورق المرحاض (مذ) 33
ورقة (نبات) (م) 7
وزة (م) 24
وسادة (م) 34
وسادة واقية (م) 21
وقت (مذ) 45
ولد (مذ) 5
ي
يخت (مذ) 37
يد (م) 4
يسروع (م) 37

قلب (مذ) 40
قلعة (م) 35
قلعة رملية (م) 27
قلم رصاص (مذ) 13
قلم لباد (مذ) 13
قميص (مذ) 32
قنديل البحر (مذ) 27
قنطرة (م) 25
قوقع (مذ) 7
قيثارة (م) 23
ك
كبير / كبيرة (مذ/م) 42
كتاب قصص (مذ) 10
كرة (م) 26
الكرة الأرضية (م) 10
كرسي (مذ) 19
كرسي قابل للطي (مذ) 26
كريم شمس (مذ) 26
كعب (مذ) 11
كعك (مذ) 29
كعكة محلاة (م) 18
كلب (مذ) 7, 36
كنزة صوفية (م) 32
كنغر (مذ) 30
كنيسة (م) 8
كهف (مذ) 17
كوال (مذ) 30
كوب (مذ) 20
كيك (مذ) 29
ل
لاعب / لاعبة خفة (مذ/م) 36
لاعب / لاعبة كرة قدم (مذ/م) 14
لسان (مذ) 5
لعبة (م) 22
لعبة القطار (م) 22
لعبة تركيب الصور (م) 22
لوحة مفاتيح (حاسوبية) (م) 11
لوحة مفاتيح (موسيقية) (م) 23
م
مارد (مذ) 35
ماصة (م) 29
ماعز (مذ) 37, 24
مائدة (م) 21
مثلث (مذ) 40
مجراف (مذ) 26
مجسم الصوت (مذ) 21
محل (مذ) 8
مختلف/ مختلفة (مذ/م) 43
مخدة (م) 21
مخروط (مذ) 41
مدخنة (م) 6
مدرسة (م) 10
مرأب (مذ) 6
مرآة (م) 33
مربع (مذ) 40
مربى (م) 18
مرتفع/مرتفعة (مذ/م) 42
مرجوحة (م) 26
مرحاض (مذ) 33
مرشة الاغتسال (م) 33
مرفق (مذ) 4
مزمار (مذ) 23
مستطيل/ مستطيلة (مذ/م) 40
مسدس (مذ) 41
مسطرة (م) 11
مسعف/ مسعفة (مذ/م) 15
مسمار (مذ) 37
مشروب (مذ) 29
مشمس (مذ) 44
مصباح (مذ) 34
المصباح السحري (مذ) 35
مُضاء (مذ) 43
مضلع (مذ) 40
مطير (مذ) 44
مُظلم (مذ) 43

صورة زيتية (م) 13
صولجان (مذ) 28
ض
ضابط شرطة (مذ) 14
ضبابي (مذ) 44
ط
طائرة (م) 9
طائرة مروحية (م) 36, 9
طاسة (م) 20
طاهي/ طاهية (مذ/م) 15
طاولة (م) 21
طباخ (مذ) 15
طباشير (م) 10
طبق (مذ) 20
طبق الفنجان (مذ) 21
طبل (مذ) 23
طبيب بيطري/طبيبة بيطرية (مذ/م) 14
طبيب/ طبيبة (مذ/م) 14
طحلب بحري (مذ) 27
طماطم (م) 19
طويل/ طويلة (مذ/م) 43
طيار (مذ) 15
ظ
ظهر (مذ) 4
ع
عاصف (مذ) 44
عربة (م) 37
عربة البضائع (م) 18
عشر/ عشرة (مذ/م) 38
عشرون (مذ & م) 39
عصا الساحر (م) 28
عظمة (م) 16
علبة الغداء (م) 10
عملات معدنية (م) 17
عمود الإنارة (مذ) 8
عنكبوت (مذ) 7
عنزة (م) 24, 37
عنق (مذ) 5
عواتق (م) 4
عين (م) 5
غ
غائم (مذ) 44
غابة (م) 25
غراء (مذ) 13
غسالة كهربائية (م) 20
غطاء (مذ) 34
غلاية (م) 20
غواص/ غواصة (مذ/م) 15
ف
فأر (حيوان) (مذ) 36, 31
فأرة (حاسب) (م) 11
فارغ/ فارغة (مذ/م) 42
فانلة (م) 33
فترة الغداء (م) 20
فترة اللعب (م) 22
فرس النهر (مذ) 30
فرشاة الرسم (م) 13
فرشة أسنان (م) 33
فرعون (مذ) 17
فرن الطبخ (مذ) 20
فزاعة (م) 25
فظ (مذ) 31
فم (مذ) 5
فيل (مذ) 30
فيل البحر (مذ) 31
ق
قبعة حفلة (م) 28
قدر (مذ) 20
قدم (م) 4
قديم/ قديمة (مذ/م) 42
قذر/ قذرة (مذ/م) 42
قرد (مذ) 30
قرنفلي/ قرنفلية (اللون) (مذ/م) 12
قصير/ قصيرة (مذ/م) 43
قط/ قطة (مذ/م) 7

ردف (م) 4
رسائل (م) 7
رسم كهفي (مذ) 17
رصاصي (اللون) (مذ) 12
رصيف (مذ) 8
رطب/ رطبة (مذ/م) 43
رقبة (م) 5
ركبة (م) 4
رمادي/ رمادية (اللون) (مذ/م) 12
ز
زبادي (مذ) 19
زرافة (م) 30
زهرة (م) 7
زهري (اللون) (مذ) 12
س
سائق حافلة (مذ) 14
سائق قطار (مذ) 15
ساحة لعب (م) 8
ساخن/ ساخنة (مذ/م) 42
ساعة يد (م) 37
ساعي البريد (مذ) 14
سبع عشر/ سبعة عشر (مذ/م) 39
سبع/ سبعة (مذ/م) 38
سبورة (م) 10
ست عشر/ ستة عشر (مذ/م) 39
ست/ ستة (مذ/م) 38
ستائر (م) 34
سترة (م) 32
ستيجوصور (مذ) 16
سجق (م) 18
سراويل داخلية (م) 32
سراويل قصيرة (م) 32
سرطان البحر (مذ) 27
سروال (مذ) 32
سرير (مذ) 34
سريع/ سريعة (مذ/م) 43
سعيد/ سعيدة (مذ/م) 43
سفينة (م) 27
سقف (مذ) 6
سكين (مذ) 20
سلة المهملات (م) 6
سلم (مذ) 6
سمكة (م) 30, 36
سياج (مذ) 6
سيارة (م) 9
سيارة إسعاف (م) 9
سيارة إطفاء (م) 9
سيارة سباق (م) 22
ش
شاحنة (م) 9
شارع (مذ) 8
شباك (مذ) 6
شبيه/ شبيهة (مذ/م) 43
شجرة (م) 7
شطيرة (م) 29
شعر (مذ) 4
شكل خماسي (مذ) 40
شكل سداسي (مذ) 41
شمعة (م) 28
شوكة (م) 20
شوكولاتة (م) 29
ص
صابون (مذ) 33
صابونة (م) 33
صافرة ورقية (م) 28
صبي (مذ) 5
صبية (م) 5
صدر (الجسم) (مذ) 4
صدفة (م) 27
صغير/ صغيرة (مذ/م) 42
صفر (مذ) 38
صمغ (مذ) 13
صَنج (م) 23
الصندوق (مذ) 18
صندوق الزبالة (مذ) 10